LIFE'S LITTLE BLUEBERRY COOKBOOK:

101 Blueberry Recipes

by Joan Bestwick

Life's Little Blueberry Cookbook
101 Blueberry Recipes

by Joan Bestwick

Copyright 2005
by Avery Color Studios, Inc.
ISBN# 1-892384-32-9
Library of Congress Control Number: 2005928681
First Edition 2005

Published by
Avery Color Studios, Inc.
Gwinn, Michigan 49841

Cover photo by Michael Prokopowicz
Michael's Photographics, Gwinn, Michigan

Proudly printed in U.S.A.

Table of Contents

I would like to thank Jesus Christ for all he has given to me and my family. All my brothers and sisters throughout Michigan and the USA who do Prison Ministry, especially Mary Engle and Norene Snow.

My friends Margie Straka, Lori Lick, Big Job, Little Job Kakish, Tony Kakish, Carman Bays, Pastor Gary and Michelle Smith, Pastor Jan Abram, Glen and Michelle McCabe, Charlie Kennedy, Connie Baginski, John and Shirley Hering, Judy and Randy Hompstead, Alice Fuhrman, Don and Patty Nueman, Brenda and Breanna Schmanski and Eric Owens. My niece Holly Manning and God child Melody Manning.

Most of all to a woman who through Jesus put my husband and I together, Sharon Rockwell, I love you more than you will ever know, you're beautiful.

*H*ello,

Blueberries are my son Michael's favorite fruit right now. We have a secret spot where we pick blueberries and it was a good year for them. Michael does well picking for a kid and will last about an hour, then suddenly the bugs make him their target and playing with sticks is more important than filling his coffee can.

Greg, Michael and I love to play in the kitchen. You never know what is going to come out of it. If it does not blow up like a science project we are doing well. But we have fun and that is worth it, to laugh as a family and do things together. Cooking is a pleasure and hobby for us and it is fun to watch Michael be creative experimenting in the kitchen.

Can you believe this is the 6th book? Thank you Avery Color Studios for this honor, you have been so good to our family. God bless you and everyone else who reads and uses these cookbooks.

All our love,
The Bestwick Family

Blueberries

Blueberries are a relative of the cranberry and are native to the United States. Blueberries were probably the first snack food consumed in North America. Native Americans used to sun dry and smoke them to store for the winter months. It is also related to the European bilberry and whortleberry.

Blueberry Facts

Blueberries have 80 calories per cup. Blueberries provide about 5 grams of fiber per cup and are a source of Vitamin C.

How to buy and store blueberries

When looking for blueberries, they should be firm and dry. The skin should be smooth and deep purple-blue.

Fresh blueberries can be stored from 10 and 14 days and they need to be washed before serving.

The secret to successful blueberry freezing is to use berries that are unwashed and completely dry. There are two ways to freeze blueberries, the first is to spread the berries in a single layer on a cookie sheet and freeze solid. Transfer frozen berries to plastic bags. The second way is to simply place in a container with plastic wrap, a freezer bag or airtight container and place in freezer. They also can be canned or dehydrated per directions.

APPETIZERS
& BEVERAGES

Never give up on anybody.
Miracles happen everyday!

Cream Cheese Fruit Pizza
From the one and only Michael, the pizza king.

Crust:
1 cup margarine
1/2 cup brown sugar
1/2 cup oatmeal
2 cups flour

Filling:
12 ounces cream cheese
2 tablespoons sugar
1 teaspoon vanilla
Fresh fruits, sliced except the blueberries. Fruits to use if desired: blueberries, peaches, nectarines, strawberries, bananas and kiwi.

Mix the crust ingredients and pat into a 9 x 13 inch pan. Bake at 375° for 8-15 minutes. Mix the filling ingredients and spread over the crust right before serving. Add fruit to the top and serve.

Yummy Fruit Platter

1 8-ounce package cream cheese, softened
1/2 cup milk
2 tablespoons lemon juice
4 teaspoons sugar
1/4 teaspoon salt
1 medium honeydew, cubed
1-1/2 cups strawberries, halved
1-1/2 cups watermelon, cubed
1 cup blueberries
1 medium banana, cut into 1 inch pieces
2 medium ripe peaches, sliced
clusters of grapes

In a small mixing bowl, beat the cream cheese. Add the milk, lemon juice, sugar and salt, beat until smooth. Transfer to a small serving bowl. On a large serving platter arrange your fruits. Place your dip in the center and serve.

Pretzel Pizza
One of Michael's recipes.

3 cups finely crushed pretzels
2/3 cup sugar
1-1/4 cups butter or margarine
1 14-ounce can sweetened condensed milk
1/4 cup lime juice
1 tablespoon grated lime peel
1-1/2 cups whipped topping
7 to 8 cups fresh fruit: blueberries, strawberries, kiwi, mandarin oranges, pineapple tidbits, grapes, peaches or plums

In a bowl, combine the pretzels and sugar. Mix well. Cut in butter until mixture resembles coarse crumbs. Press into a 14 inch pizza pan. Bake at 375° for 8-10 minutes. Cool on a wire rack. Refrigerate crust for 30 minutes. Meanwhile in a bowl, combine milk, lime juice and peel. Fold in whipped topping and spread over the crust. Cover and chill. Top with fruit before serving. Serves 8.

Fruit Pizza

This is another one of Michael's, as you can see, pizza is his thing.

1 sheet refrigerated pie pastry
1 cup water
1 8-ounce package vanilla pudding mix
1 3-ounce package lemon gelatin
1 8-ounce package cream cheese
2 tablespoons sugar
1/2 cup or more Cool Whip®
1 cup quartered fresh strawberries
1 cup blueberries
1 cup kiwi fruit, sliced
1 8-ounce can pineapple chunks, drained

On a lightly floured surface, roll pastry into a 12 inch circle. Transfer to a 14 inch pizza pan. Pick pastry with a fork. Bake at 450° for 6-8 minutes or until golden brown. Cool on a wire rack. In a saucepan combine the water and pudding mix until smooth. Bring to a boil over medium heat stirring constantly. Whisk in gelatin. Cook and stir 1 minute longer or until thickened. Remove from heat and let cool. In a small mixing bowl, cream the cheese and sugar. Fold in the whipped topping. Spread the cream cheese mixture over the crust to within 1/2 inch of the edges. Spread gelatin mixture over the cream cheese mixture. Arrange fruit over the top. Chill. Refrigerate leftovers.

Fruit and Limeade

2 bananas, sliced
1 cup blueberries
1 cup strawberries
Some watermelon chunks
2 tablespoons frozen limeade concentrate thawed. You can use more if
desired.

Place the fruit in a bowl. Pour the limeade over the fruit and gently stir. Chill and serve.

Blueberry Smoothies

1 ripe medium banana
3/4 cup blueberries
1/4 cup vanilla yogurt (or ice cream)
3/4 cup milk
1/2 cup crushed ice

Measure and combine all ingredients into a blender. On high speed mix until smooth or you hear no more ice sounds. Makes 1 serving.

Berry Smoothies

2-1/2 cups orange juice
1 cup raspberry sherbet
1 large frozen banana, sliced
1 cup frozen strawberries
1 cup frozen blueberries

In a blender, combine all the ingredients in the order listed. Cover and process for 30 seconds or until smooth. Stir if necessary. Pour into chilled glasses, serve immediately. Serves 5, one cup servings.

JAMS & SAUCES

Forbidden fruits create many jams.

Blueberry Jam

4-1/2 cups fresh blueberries, slightly crushed
7 cups sugar
2 tablespoons lemon juice
2 teaspoons butter
2 3-ounce packages liquid pectin

Combine blueberries, sugar, lemon juice and butter in a large Dutch oven. Bring to a rolling boil. Boil for 1 minute, stirring constantly. Remove from heat and immediately stir in pectin. Stir and alternately skim off foam with a metal spoon for 5 minutes. Quickly pour into hot sterilized jars, leaving 1/4 inch headspace. Cover with hot lids and screw on bands. Process in boiling water bath for 10 minutes.

Spiced Blueberry Jam

1-1/2 quarts blueberries
2 tablespoons lemon juice
1/4 teaspoon cloves
1/4 teaspoon cinnamon
1/4 teaspoon allspice
1 1-3/4-ounce powder fruit pectin
5 cups sugar

Sterilize 8, 6-ounce jelly jars. Keep them in hot water until ready to fill. Wash and drain blueberries. Puree the blueberries in a blender or food processor. You need 1 quart of puree. In a large pan combine puree, lemon juice, cloves, cinnamon, allspice and fruit pectin. Stir to mix well. Over high heat, bring mixture to a full rolling boil. Boil for 1 minute stirring constantly. Add sugar all at once. Again, bring to a rolling boil and boil for 1 minute, stirring constantly. Skim off the foam on top of the jam. Ladle into hot sterilized jelly jars and seal.

Blueberry Rhubarb Jam

3 cups rhubarb, finely cut
3 cups blueberries, crushed
7 cups sugar
1 bottle liquid fruit pectin

Combine rhubarb and blueberries in a large saucepan, add sugar and mix. Place over high heat and bring to a full rolling boil for 1 minute, stirring constantly. Remove from heat and add the pectin. Stir and skim foam for 5 minutes. Ladle into hot sterilized jars and seal with lids and rings. To seal, place in a hot water bath for 5 minutes.

Blueberry Rhubarb Jam, Version 2

1 quart rhubarb, cut into 1/2 inch slices
1 quart blueberries
6 cups sugar

Put all ingredients into a heavy medium saucepan over medium-high heat. Bring to a boil, stirring until thick. Pour into hot sterilized jars and seal.

Spiced Blueberries

3 quarts blueberries
1 cup vinegar
1 cup sugar
2 tablespoons whole cloves

Combine all the ingredients in a large pot and bring to a boil. Simmer, stirring often until the liquid begins to jell, about 20-25 minutes. Pour this mixture into hot jars, top with lids and rings. Place in a hot water bath for 5 minutes. Makes 2 pints.

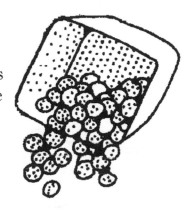

Blueberry Sauce

1/4 cup sugar
2 tablespoons cornstarch
1-1/2 cups water
2 teaspoons lemon juice
1-1/3 cups fresh blueberries or 12-ounces frozen blueberries

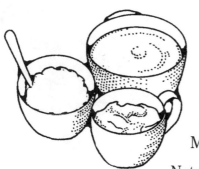

In a saucepan, thoroughly combine the sugar and cornstarch. Stir in the 1-1/2 cups of water, lemon juice and blueberries. Cook the mixture, stirring over medium heat until it comes to a boil. It will become thickened and translucent after about 5-6 minutes. Makes 2 cups.

Note: If you are using frozen blueberries, drain the berries, reserving the juice. Add enough water to the juice to measure 1-1/2 cups of liquid, use in place of the 1-1/2 cups water.

Gingered Blueberry Sauce

1/2 cup granulated sugar
4 teaspoons cornstarch
1/2 to 1 tablespoon fresh ginger root, grated
pinch of salt if desired
2/3 cup cold water
2 cups fresh blueberries
1 tablespoon fresh lemon juice

In a small saucepan stir together sugar, cornstarch, ginger root and salt. Gradually stir in the water, cook over medium heat, stirring constantly until mixture thickens and comes to a boil. Stir in the blueberries and lemon juice, reduce heat and simmer on low for 5 minutes until the berries are tender. Serve immediately or let cool, cover and refrigerate up to 3 days. Serve hot over crepes, pound cake, waffles or cold over ice cream.

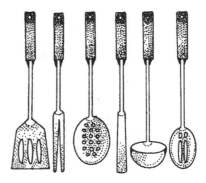

Blueberry Sauce For Cake

2 pints fresh strawberries, hulled
1 pint fresh blueberries
1/3 cup sugar
1 tablespoon lemon juice
1/2 teaspoon almond extract
1 yellow cake, pound cake or angel food cake

In a food processor pulse 1 pint strawberries to a coarse puree. Pour into a large bowl. Slice remaining strawberries and add to the bowl along with 1/2 of the blueberries. In a small saucepan, combine the remaining blueberries, sugar and lemon juice. Bring this mixture to a boil over high heat, stirring and crushing some of the berries with the back of your spoon. Cook until the sugar dissolves and the juices become syrupy, about 3 minutes. Pour blueberry sauce into the bowl with the strawberry mixture. Stir in the almond extract. Cool to room temperature or refrigerate up to 8 hours. To serve, cut cake into slices and spoon berry sauce on top. Top with Cool Whip® or ice cream if desired.

Easy Blueberry Sauce

1 14-1/2-ounce can blueberries
2 tablespoons light corn syrup

Drain the blueberry liquid into a small saucepan. Stir in the corn
syrup. Bring this to a boil over medium-high heat, simmer for 10 minutes.
Stir the blueberries into this mixture. Serve warm. Serve on ice cream,
pancakes or cakes.

Blueberry Glaze

1 10-ounce package frozen blueberries, thawed
2 tablespoons sugar
2 tablespoons cornstarch
1 tablespoon lemon juice

Drain your blueberries reserving 1/2 cup of the berry liquid. In a saucepan combine the sugar and cornstarch. Add the 1/2 cup blueberry liquid, stirring until smooth. Bring this to a boil, stirring over medium heat and boil for 1 minute. The mixture will be thick and translucent. Remove from the heat, let cool slightly. Add the lemon juice and blueberries. Cool completely before spreading over the top of a cooled cheesecake. Makes 1 cup.

Blueberry Syrup

2 cups blueberries
1/2 cup sugar
1/2 cup water
1 teaspoon lemon juice

Place all ingredients in a heavy pan.
Over medium-low heat bring to a
simmer, cooking for 10 to 20 minutes.
Makes 2-1/2 cups.

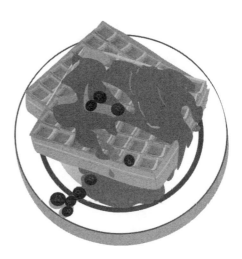

BREAKFAST FAVORITES

Do not be overcome by evil,
but overcome evil with good. Romans 12:21

Blueberry Sour Cream Pancakes

1-1/3 cups unsifted flour
1/2 teaspoon baking soda
1 teaspoon salt
1 tablespoon sugar
1/4 teaspoon nutmeg
1 egg, beaten
1 cup sour cream
1 cup milk
2 teaspoons oil
1/4 cup melted butter
1 cup blueberries

In a bowl, combine the dry ingredients thoroughly. In another bowl combine the egg, sour cream, milk, oil and melted butter. Blend this into the flour mixture until lumpy. Mix in the blueberries. With a spoon or ladle, drop batter onto a hot greased griddle or non-stick pan. Cook until bubbles appear on the surface. Turn pancake and cook until golden brown. Remove the pancake from the griddle. Makes 10-12 pancakes.

Fruit Crepes

2 egg whites
2/3 cup milk
2 teaspoons vegetable oil
1/2 cup flour
1/4 teaspoon salt
1/4 cup orange marmalade
1 cup blueberries
8 teaspoons sugar
1/2 cup sour cream
1/8 teaspoon ground cinnamon

In a mixing bowl, combine egg whites, milk and oil. Combine flour and salt. Add to milk mixture and mix well. In saucepan heat marmalade until melted, remove from heat. Fold in the berries and sugar. Set aside. In a small bowl combine sour cream and cinnamon. Set aside. Heat an 8 inch nonstick skillet and coat with nonstick cooking spray. Add 2 tablespoons batter. Lift and tilt the pan to evenly coat the bottom. Cook until top appears dry and bottom is lightly brown. Remove to a wire rack. Repeat with remaining batter. Spread each crepe with 1 tablespoon sour cream mixture. Roll up and place in an 11 x 7 x 2 inch baking dish. Spoon fruit mixture over the top. Bake uncovered at 375° for 15 minutes.

Blueberry Scones

3 cups buttermilk baking mix
2 tablespoons sugar
1 cup blueberries
1/4 cup milk
2 eggs

Glaze:
1 egg, well beaten
2 tablespoons sugar

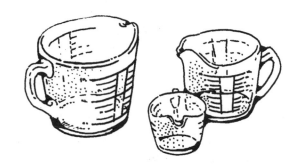

Preheat oven to 400°. Combine baking mix, 2 tablespoons sugar and blueberries. Pour milk in measuring cup. Add the eggs to the milk and beat with a fork until well mixed. Stir liquid into baking mix until moistened. Turn dough onto a lightly floured work surface and pat into a 9 inch round about 1/2 inch thick. Brush dough with beaten egg and sprinkle with sugar. Cut round into 12 wedges. Place on ungreased cookie sheet and bake for 10-12 minutes until golden. Serve with butter and jam.

Blueberry Pecan Waffles

This recipe is from my sister-in-law Peggy Manning.

1-1/2 cups all-purpose flour
1 teaspoon baking powder
1/2 teaspoon salt
2 eggs, separated
1 cup milk
1/4 cup butter or margarine, melted
1/8 cup finely chopped pecans or walnuts
1/2 cup blueberries

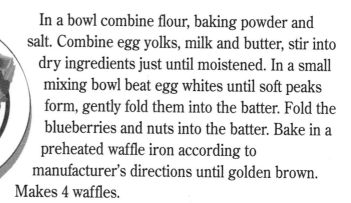

In a bowl combine flour, baking powder and salt. Combine egg yolks, milk and butter, stir into dry ingredients just until moistened. In a small mixing bowl beat egg whites until soft peaks form, gently fold them into the batter. Fold the blueberries and nuts into the batter. Bake in a preheated waffle iron according to manufacturer's directions until golden brown. Makes 4 waffles.

Fruit Filled Puff Pancake

1 tablespoon butter
1/3 cup flour
3 tablespoons sugar, divided
1/4 teaspoon salt
3 eggs, beaten
1/2 cup milk
1-1/2 cups fresh or frozen blueberries
1 medium ripe banana, sliced
1/4 teaspoon ground cinnamon

Place butter in a 9 inch pie plate. Bake at 400° for 4-5 minutes or until melted. Meanwhile in a bowl combine the flour, 1 tablespoon sugar and salt. Add eggs and milk, whisk until smooth. Pour into hot pie plate. Bake at 400° for 10 to 12 minutes or until edges are puffed and golden brown. Meanwhile combine blueberries and banana. In a small bowl combine cinnamon and remaining sugar. Spoon fruit mixture into pancake. Sprinkle with cinnamon sugar. Cut into wedges. Serve immediately. Serves 4.

Blueberry Fritters

2 tablespoons flour
1 cup fresh blueberries
1 cup flour
2-1/2 teaspoons baking powder
1/4 cup sugar
pinch of salt
1 egg, beaten
1/3 cup milk
vegetable oil
powdered sugar

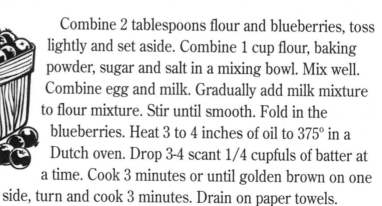

Combine 2 tablespoons flour and blueberries, toss lightly and set aside. Combine 1 cup flour, baking powder, sugar and salt in a mixing bowl. Mix well. Combine egg and milk. Gradually add milk mixture to flour mixture. Stir until smooth. Fold in the blueberries. Heat 3 to 4 inches of oil to 375° in a Dutch oven. Drop 3-4 scant 1/4 cupfuls of batter at a time. Cook 3 minutes or until golden brown on one side, turn and cook 3 minutes. Drain on paper towels. Sprinkle with powdered sugar. Makes 1 dozen.

Blueberry Flapjacks

3 eggs
1 cup sifted flour
3 teaspoons baking powder
1/2 teaspoon salt
2 teaspoons granulated sugar
1 teaspoon light brown sugar
1/2 cup buttermilk
2 tablespoons butter, melted
1-1/2 cups blueberries

In a large bowl, beat eggs until light and fluffy with a mixer on high speed about 2 minutes. Add flour, baking powder, salt and granulated sugar. Add the brown sugar and beat until smooth. Stir in the buttermilk and butter just until combined. Do not over beat. Fold in the blueberries. Slowly heat a well oiled griddle or skillet. To test the temperature of the pan drop some water on the pan and if it is hot enough the water should roll off in droplets. Use 1/4 cup of batter for each flapjack. Cook until bubbles form on the surface and the edges become dry. Turn and cook 2 minutes longer or until brown, then serve.

Blueberry Lemon Crepes

Crepes:
1/2 cup biscuit mix
1 egg
6 tablespoons milk

Filling:
1 3-ounce package cream cheese, softened
1-1/2 cups half-and-half
1 tablespoon lemon juice
1 3-3/4 ounce package lemon instant pudding

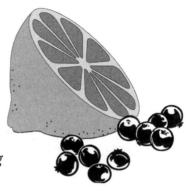

Topping:
1 cup blueberry pie filling

Lightly grease a 6-7 inch skillet, heat until hot. Beat crepe ingredients together until smooth, for each crepe pour 2 tablespoons batter into the skillet. Quickly rotate skillet until the batter covers the skillet bottom. Cook only until golden brown on each side. Stack the crepes with a paper towel between them. Crepes may be made in advance and refrigerated, tightly covered until needed. Meanwhile, make the filling by beating the cream cheese, half-and-half, lemon juice and dry pudding. Mix on low speed with mixer until well blended, about 2 minutes. Refrigerate at least 30 minutes. Spoon about 2 tablespoons of pudding mixture onto each crepe and roll up. Top with remaining pudding mixture. Garnish with blueberry pie filling.

Blueberry Applesauce Fritters

2 eggs, beaten
1/2 cup applesauce
1/4 cup sugar
1/4 cup milk
1/4 cup butter or margarine, melted
1/2 teaspoon baking soda
1/2 teaspoon ground cinnamon
1/2 teaspoon lemon extract
1 cup flour
1 cup blueberries, extra optional for garnish

In a large bowl combine eggs, applesauce, sugar, milk, melted butter, baking soda, cinnamon and lemon extract. Add the flour, stir until just combined. Fold in one cup blueberries. Pour about 2 tablespoons batter onto a hot, lightly greased skillet. Cook over medium heat about 2 minutes on each side or until fritters are golden brown. Turn when fritters have bubbly surfaces and edges are slightly dry. Serve fritters topped with whipped cream and additional blueberries. 6 servings.

Blueberry Popover Pancake

1 cup blueberries
1 cup milk
2 tablespoons butter, melted
2 eggs
1 teaspoon vanilla
1/4 teaspoon salt
1/4 teaspoon nutmeg
1/4 cup sugar
1 cup flour
1/4 cup sugar mixed with 1 teaspoon ground cinnamon

Preheat the oven to 450°. Butter a 9 inch pie plate and place the blueberries into the pan. Combine the milk, butter, eggs and vanilla in a blender or food processor. Pulse on and off several times to blend the mixture. Add the salt, nutmeg, 1/4 cup sugar and flour. Mix and process until the mixture is smooth. Pour over the berries and sprinkle with 2 teaspoons of cinnamon sugar. Bake for 20 minutes. Reduce the oven to 350° and bake until the pancake is golden brown, about 15 to 20 minutes. Cut into wedges and serve immediately.

FRUIT BOWLS
& SALADS

Lazy hands make a man poor,
but diligent hands bring wealth. Proverbs 10:4

Tortilla Fruit Bowls

4 7 inch to 8 inch flour tortillas
2 tablespoons butter or margarine, melted
2 tablespoons sugar
1/4 teaspoon ground cinnamon
1 cup strawberries, halved
1 cup blueberries
2 cups honeydew melon, cubed
1 large orange, peeled and sectioned
1/4 cup orange marmalade
whipped topping
orange slices

Place 4 small ovenproof bowls or 20 oz. individual casserole, each 5 or 6 inches wide. Brush both sides of the flour tortillas with melted butter. Press tortillas into the bowls forming a cup. Combine the sugar and cinnamon and sprinkle over the tortilla cups. Bake in a 350° oven for 20 minutes or until tortillas are lightly browned and crisp. Remove tortillas from the bowls and cool on wire racks. In a large bowl combine the fruits and drain off any liquid if any. Gently stir in the marmalade, tossing to coat. Place tortilla cups on individual plates and spoon in the fruit. Garnish with whipped topping and orange slices.

Maple Lime Syrup Fruit Bowl

1/2 cup water
1/4 cup lime juice
1/4 cup honey
1/4 cup maple syrup
2 cups blueberries
2 cups strawberries, halved
2 cups raspberries
1-1/2 cups seedless green grapes, halved
4 medium bananas
whipped cream

In a small saucepan combine the water, lime juice, honey and maple syrup. Heat and stir until combined. Cool. In a large bowl combine the blueberries, strawberries, raspberries and grapes. Pour the syrup over the fruit and toss gently. Cover and chill for 1-2 hours stirring gently a couple of times. Just before serving, slice bananas and stir into the fruit. Serve if desire with whipped cream. Serves 10-12.

Endless Fruit Medley

1 20-ounce can pineapple chunks, undrained
1 11-ounce can mandarin oranges, drained
1 or 2 navel oranges, peeled and chopped
1 large red apple, cored and cubed
1 cup fresh strawberries
1 cup red seedless grapes, halved
3 kiwi fruit, peeled and sliced
1 cup blueberries
1 cup dark sweet cherries, pitted
2 medium firm bananas, sliced

In a large bowl combine the first 7 ingredients and gently mix. Cover and refrigerate overnight. Just before serving fold in the blueberries, cherries and banana. Gently toss, serves 10.

Melon Blueberry Cup

1 cup cantaloupe or honeydew melon, cubed
1 cup blueberries
1 cup pineapple chunks
1/2 cup sugar, optional

In a bowl, combine fruits. Chill for an hour. Serve in small bowls. Top with a sprinkle of sugar if desired.

Honey Lime Fruit Salad

1 20-ounce can unsweetened pineapple chunks
1 11-ounce can mandarin oranges, drained
2 cups fresh strawberries, sliced
1 medium banana, cut into 1/4 inch slices
1 cup blueberries
2 kiwi fruit, peeled, halved and sliced
2 tablespoons lime juice
1 tablespoon honey
1/4 teaspoon grated lime peel

Drain pineapple, reserving 1/4 cup juice, set aside. In a bowl combine the fruit. In a small bowl combine the lime juice, honey, lime peel and reserved pineapple juice. Pour over the fruit and gently toss to coat. Makes 6 servings.

Fruit Cottage Cheese Salad
With Honey Ginger Dressing

Salad:
1 16-ounce container cottage cheese
lettuce leaves
1 cup blueberries
1 large peach
2 medium bananas, sliced
coarsely chopped salted or toasted nuts

Honey ginger dressing:
1/4 cup vegetable oil
1/4 cup lime juice
1/4 cup honey
2 tablespoons mayonnaise
1/4 teaspoon salt
1/4 teaspoon ground ginger

Place all ingredients into a tightly covered container and shake well.

Arrange lettuce leaves on four salad plates. Spoon cottage cheese on each plate. Arrange fruit on top and sprinkle with dressing.

Creamy Fruit Salad

1 20-ounce can pineapple chunks
1 11-ounce can mandarin oranges
1 3-ounce package cook and serve vanilla pudding mix
1 cup fresh strawberries, sliced
1/2 cup maraschino cherries
1 cup blueberries
1 banana, sliced

Drain pineapple and oranges, reserving juices in a 2 cup measuring cup. Set fruit aside. Add enough water to the juices to measure 1-1/2 cups. In a saucepan whisk the juices and pudding mix. Cook and stir over medium heat until mixture comes to a full boil. Cool to room temperature, stirring occasionally. Fold in the fruit except the banana, cover and refrigerate. Just before serving, fold in the sliced banana. Serves 6-8.

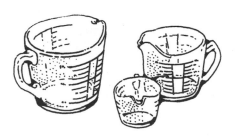

Large Tropical Fruit Salad

2 large bananas, sliced
4 teaspoons lemon juice
2 large cantaloupe melons, cubed
5 cups fresh pineapple, cubed
3 cups fresh strawberries, halved
2 cups blueberries
1 cup whipping cream
1/2 cup confectioners sugar
1/2 cup flaked coconut, toasted
2 tablespoons slivered almonds, toasted

In a 4 quart serving bowl, toss the bananas and lemon juice. Stir in the cantaloupe, pineapple, strawberries and blueberries. In a small mixing bowl beat cream until it begins to thicken and add sugar. Beat until soft peaks form. Spoon over fruit. Sprinkle with coconut and almonds. Serve immediately. Yields 16-20 servings.

MUFFINS & BREAD

God gave us two ears and one mouth. We should listen twice as much as we talk. Dr. Joanne Root-Bliss

Blueberry Streusel Muffins

1 cup milk
1/4 cup vegetable oil
1/2 teaspoon vanilla
1 large egg
2 cups flour
1/3 cup sugar
3 teaspoons baking powder
1/2 teaspoon salt
1 cup fresh blueberries

Streusel Topping:
2 tablespoons margarine or butter
1/4 cup flour
2 tablespoons packed brown sugar
1/4 teaspoon ground cinnamon

Preheat oven to 400°. Grease the bottoms of 12 medium muffin cups or line cups with paper baking cups. Prepare the streusel topping. In a medium bowl, cut the margarine into the flour, brown sugar and cinnamon until the mixture is crumbly. Set aside. In a mixing bowl beat the milk, oil, vanilla and egg. Stir in the flour, sugar, baking powder and salt all at once just until flour is moistened. Batter will be lumpy. Fold in the blueberries. Divide the batter evenly among muffin cups. Sprinkle each with about 2 teaspoons topping. Bake 20 to 25 minutes or until golden brown. Immediately remove muffins from pan to wire rack.

Blueberry Bran Muffins

1-1/2 cups bran cereal
1 cup buttermilk
1 egg beaten
1/4 cup melted butter
1 cup flour
1/3 cup brown sugar
2 teaspoons baking powder
1/2 teaspoon baking soda
1/2 teaspoon salt
1 cup blueberries

Combine bran cereal and buttermilk, let stand 3 minutes or until liquid is absorbed. Stir in egg and melted butter, set aside. In a different bowl, stir together the flour, brown sugar, baking powder, baking soda and salt. Add bran mixture stirring until just moistened. Fold in the blueberries. Fill 12 greased muffin cups 2/3 full. Bake at 400° for 20-25 minutes.

Blueberry Tea Muffins

1-3/4 cups sifted cake flour
1-1/2 teaspoons baking powder
1/4 teaspoon salt
1/3 cup butter or margarine
1/2 cup sugar
1 egg, well beaten
1/2 cup milk
3/4 cup fresh blueberries, lightly floured

Preheat oven to 400°. Sift the flour, baking powder and salt. In a bowl, cream the butter with a mixer until light in color. Add the sugar, beating until fluffy. Add the egg beating until smooth. Add the dry ingredients alternately with the milk. Beat after each addition, until smooth. Add the blueberries by folding them in. Fill greased muffin tins 2/3 full. Bake for about 30 minutes.

Crumb-Topped Blueberry Muffins

4 cups flour
1 cup sugar
6 teaspoons baking powder
1/2 teaspoon salt
1 cup cold butter
2 eggs, lightly beaten
1-1/3 cups milk
2 teaspoons grated orange peel
2 teaspoons vanilla extract
2 cups fresh blueberries

Topping:
1/4 cup sugar
3 tablespoons flour
1/4 teaspoon ground cinnamon
2 tablespoons cold butter

In a bowl, combine the flour, sugar, baking powder and salt. Cut in butter until mixture resembles coarse crumbs. Combine the eggs, milk, orange peel and extract, stir into crumb mixture just until moistened. Gently fold in blueberries, batter will be stiff. Fill paper lined or greased muffin cups 2/3s full. Topping: In a bowl, combine the sugar, flour and cinnamon. Cut in the butter until mixture resembles coarse crumbs. Sprinkle about 1 teaspoon over each muffin. Bake at 375° for 20-25 minutes or until a toothpick comes out clean. Cool for 5 minutes before removing from pans to wire racks. Makes 2 dozen.

Blueberry Corn Muffins

1/4 cup butter or margarine, softened
1/4 cup sugar
1/4 cup packed brown sugar
1 egg
1 cup flour
1/2 cup corn meal
2 teaspoons baking powder
1/4 teaspoon salt
1/4 teaspoon ground nutmeg
1/2 cup milk
1 cup blueberries, fresh or frozen

In a mixing bowl, cream butter and sugars. Add egg, mix well. Combine the flour, corn meal, baking powder, salt and nutmeg. Add the dry mixture to the creamed mixture alternately with the milk until just moistened. Fold in the blueberries. Coat 12 muffin cups with non-stick cooking spray or use paper liners. Fill each tin 2/3s full of batter. Bake at 400° for 18-22 minutes or until a toothpick comes out clean. Cool for 5 minutes before removing muffins from pan to a wire rack to cool.

Blueberry Orange Bread

2 cups flour
1 cup sugar
1 teaspoon baking powder
1/2 teaspoon baking soda
1/2 teaspoon salt
1 egg
1/2 cup orange juice
1/3 cup water
2 tablespoons butter or margarine, melted
2 tablespoons grated orange peel
3/4 cup fresh or frozen blueberries

In a large bowl, combine the first five ingredients. In another bowl combine the egg, orange juice, water, butter and orange peel. Add to dry ingredients just until combined. Fold in the blueberries. Pour into a greased and floured 8 x 4 x 2 inch loaf pan. Bake at 350° for 65 to 70 minutes or until a toothpick inserted near the center comes out clean. Cool for 10 minutes, remove from pan to a wire rack.

CRISPS, CRUMBLES
& COBBLERS

Peace starts with a smile.

Blueberry Rhubarb Crisp

3 cups fresh or frozen blueberries, thawed
2 cups fresh or frozen sliced rhubarb, thawed
1/2 cup rolled oats
1/2 cup flour
1/2 cup packed brown sugar
1/2 teaspoon ground cinnamon
1/4 cup butter or margarine

Preheat oven to 350°. In a buttered 2 quart square baking dish place the fruit. In a bowl combine the oats, flour, brown sugar and cinnamon. With a fork cut in the butter until this mixture resembles crumbs. Sprinkle topping over the fruit. Bake for 30 to 35 minutes or until the fruit is tender and the topping is golden. Serves 6.

Fruit Crisp

1 cup quick cooking rolled oats
3/4 cup corn flake crumbs
1/2 cup packed brown sugar
1/3 cup chopped pecans
1 teaspoon ground cinnamon
1/4 cup butter or margarine, melted
2 cups apples, peeled,
  cored and thinly sliced
1 cup blueberries

1 cup pears, peeled and thinly sliced
1 cup strawberries, halved
1 cup rhubarb, sliced
1 tablespoon lemon juice
1/2 cup dried cranberries
1/2 cup packed brown sugar
3 tablespoons flour
whipped cream or vanilla ice cream

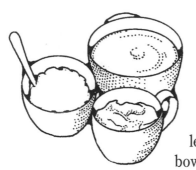

In a medium mixing bowl, combine oats, corn flake crumbs, brown sugar, pecans and cinnamon, pour melted butter or margarine over oat mixture. Stir until combined, set aside. In a large bowl, combine apples, blueberries, pears, strawberries and rhubarb. Sprinkle with lemon juice. Stir in the cranberries. In a small bowl, combine 1/2 cup brown sugar and the flour. Add to apple mixture. Toss to coat. Place apple mixture in a buttered 2 quart rectangular baking dish and cover with oat mixture. Bake in a 375° oven for 45 minutes or until apples are tender. Serve warm with whipped topping or ice cream.

Blueberry Pineapple Crisp

1-1/2 cups flaked coconut
1 cup flour
1 cup packed brown sugar
1/2 cup butter or margarine, melted
1/8 teaspoon salt

Filling:
3/4 cup sugar
3 tablespoons cornstarch
1 8-ounce can crushed pineapple, undrained
1 cup blueberries
1 tablespoon lemon juice
1 tablespoon butter or margarine

In a bowl combine the coconut, flour, brown sugar, butter and salt. Press 1-1/2 cups into a greased 9 inch square baking pan, set remaining mixture aside. In a saucepan, combine the filling ingredients. Bring to a boil, cook and stir for 2 minutes or until thickened and bubbly. Cool, spread over the crust. Sprinkle with reserved coconut mixture. Bake at 350° for 25 to 30 minutes or until golden brown. Cool on a wire rack. Makes 9 servings.

Blueberry Granola Crumble

1 pint fresh blueberries
1 tablespoon brown sugar
1 teaspoon vanilla extract
1/3 cup granola cereal
1 teaspoon hazelnut oil, optional
ice cream, frozen yogurt or Cool Whip®

Preheat oven to 400°. In a bowl, combine blueberries, brown sugar and vanilla. Toss and allow to set for 15 minutes. Take four 4-ounce ramekin dishes and divide the blueberry mixture between them. In a small bowl toss granola with hazelnut oil. Top the blueberries with granola. Place ramekins on a baking sheet. Bake for about 20 minutes or until golden brown and bubbly. Serve warm with ice cream, frozen yogurt or Cool Whip®.

Blueberry Buckle

1/2 cup shortening
1/4 cup sugar
1 egg
1 cup flour
2 teaspoons baking powder
1/4 teaspoon salt
1/2 cup milk

1 16-ounce package frozen
   blueberries, thawed and drained
2 teaspoons lemon juice
1/2 cup flour
1/4 cup sugar
1/4 cup butter or margarine, softened
1/2 teaspoon ground cinnamon

Cream the shortening with an electric mixer. Gradually add 1/4 cup sugar, beating the mixture until light and fluffy. Add egg and beat well. Combine 1 cup flour, baking powder and salt. Add to creamed mixture alternately with milk beginning and ending with flour mixture. Mix well after each addition. Spread batter into a greased 9 inch square pan. Combine blueberries and lemon juice, sprinkle over batter. Combine 1/2 cup flour, 1/4 cup sugar, butter and cinnamon, mix well. Crumble this over the blueberries. Bake at 350º for 45-55 minutes or until a wooden pick inserted comes out clean. Serve warm. Yield 9 servings.

German Blueberry Kuchen

1-1/2 cups sifted flour
2 teaspoons baking powder
1/2 teaspoon salt
3/4 cup sugar
1/4 cup soft shortening
2/3 cup milk
1 teaspoon vanilla
1/2 teaspoon grated lemon peel (1/2 lemon)
1 egg
1 cup fresh blueberries
3 tablespoons sugar
1 teaspoon grated lemon peel

Sift together flour, baking powder, salt and sugar. Add shortening, milk, vanilla and 1/2 teaspoon grated lemon peel. Beat with mixer on medium speed for 3 minutes. Add egg and beat with the mixer 2 more minutes longer. Turn the mixture into a greased 8 inch square pan. In a bowl, mix together the blueberries, 3 tablespoons sugar and 1 teaspoon grated lemon peel. Sprinkle this mixture over the batter in the pan. Bake at 350º for 40 to 50 minutes or until lightly browned. Cut into squares and serve warm.

Blueberry Rhubarb Crumble
This recipe is from one of my best friends and son's
Godmother Karen Frampton

3 cups fresh or frozen blueberries
2 cups fresh rhubarb, sliced
1/2 cup sugar
2 tablespoons flour

Toss the sugar and flour into the fruit and set aside.

1-1/2 cups rolled oats
2/3 cup brown sugar
1/2 cup flour
1/2 cup butter or margarine

Mix the oats, brown sugar and flour. Cut in the butter to resemble crumbs. Reserve 1 cup oatmeal mixture. In a 9 x 9 x 2 or 8 x 8 inch pan. Pat the remaining oatmeal mixture into the pan to form a crust. Bake crust at 350° for 10-15 minutes. Then top the crust with the fruit mixture and then sprinkle the reserved oatmeal mixture on top of fruit. Bake at 350° for 45 minutes.

Blueberry Cobbler

2 pints blueberries
1/3 cup sugar
1 tablespoon tapioca
1/2 teaspoon cinnamon
1/4 teaspoon salt
1/4 cup water
2 tablespoons butter
1 cup unsifted flour
1-1/2 teaspoons baking powder
1/4 teaspoon salt
3 tablespoons oil
6 tablespoons milk

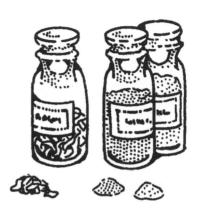

In a pot combine the blueberries, sugar, tapioca, cinnamon, 1/4 teaspoon salt, water and butter. Cook slowly until the blueberries are softened. In a bowl mix the flour, baking powder and a 1/4 teaspoon salt. Blend in the oil. Gradually add the milk to form a soft dough. Place the dough on a floured board. Roll into an 8 x 10 inch rectangle. With a sharp knife cut the dough into 1/2 inch slices. Pour blueberry mixture into a greased baking pan. Place slices of dough on top. Bake at 400° for 20 to 25 minutes until golden brown. Remove to a rack. Let stand for 5 minutes. Cut into squares. Serves 6.

Quick Blueberry Cobbler

1/2 cup flour
1/2 cup sugar
1 teaspoon baking powder
dash of salt
1/2 cup milk
2 tablespoons butter or margarine,
  cut into small pieces
2 cups blueberries
1/3 cup cranberry juice cocktail
whipped cream

In a medium bowl stir together the flour, sugar, baking powder and salt. Stir in the milk. Pour into a buttered 2 quart square baking dish or a 9 inch pie plate. Dot with butter or margarine. Sprinkle blueberries over the top. Slowly pour the cranberry juice cocktail over the fruit, do not stir. Bake in a 400° oven for 25-30 minutes or until golden brown and bubbly. Serve warm with whipped cream.

Berry Rhubarb Cobbler

2 cups rhubarb, chopped
2 cups strawberries, sliced
1 cup blueberries
1 tablespoon balsamic vinegar
1 cup sugar
2 tablespoons cornstarch
1 cup flour

3/4 cup sugar
1/3 cup sliced almonds
1/8 teaspoon salt
1 egg, beaten
1/3 cup butter or margarine, melted
whipped cream
ground nutmeg

In a large bowl stir together rhubarb, strawberries, blueberries and vinegar. Combine 1 cup sugar and cornstarch. Add this to the fruit tossing to coat. Spread the fruit in an ungreased 2 quart rectangular baking dish and set aside. In a medium bowl combine the flour, 3/4 cup sugar, almonds and salt. Stir in the egg until crumbly. Sprinkle over the fruit. Slowly drizzle melted butter over the crumb topping. Bake in a 375° oven for 35-40 minutes or until topping is golden brown. Serve with whipped topping and a little ground nutmeg on top. Serves 8.

Peach Blueberry Cobbler

2 cups fresh peaches
1/2 cup sugar
4 teaspoons quick cooking tapioca
2 teaspoons fresh lemon juice
1 cup fresh blueberries
dash of nutmeg

Cobbler:
1 cup flour
2 tablespoons sugar
1-1/2 teaspoons baking powder
1/8 teaspoon salt
1 teaspoon grated lemon rind
1/4 cup butter or margarine
1/2 cup evaporated milk

Combine the peaches, sugar, tapioca, lemon juice and blueberries in a pan over medium heat. Bring this mixture to a boil and cook for a couple of minutes until thickened. Add the nutmeg and stir, remove from the heat and place in a 1-1/2 quart baking dish. In a bowl combine the flour, sugar, baking powder, salt and lemon rind. Then add the butter. Using a fork or pastry blender, blend until the mixture resembles corn meal. Add the milk and stir until the dough is moistened and mixed. Drop by tablespoons over the hot filling. Bake at 400° for 25 to 30 minutes or until the top is golden brown. Serves 8.

Easy Blueberry Cobbler

2-1/4 cups blueberries
1/4 cup plus 2 teaspoons sugar
2 teaspoons lemon juice
2 tablespoons butter
1 cup baking mix (like Bisquick®)
1/2 cup milk

Preheat the oven to 450°. In a shallow 1 quart baking dish toss the blueberries with 1/4 cup sugar and lemon juice. Cut the butter into small pieces and scatter over the berries. Place the baking dish into the oven to heat while preparing the topping. In a medium bowl, stir the baking mix and milk together until a soft dough forms. Spoon 8 rounded tablespoons of dough onto the blueberry mixture, spacing them about 1/2 inch apart. Sprinkle the remaining 2 teaspoons of sugar over the cobbler topping. Return the cobbler to the oven and bake until the topping is golden brown and the fruit juices are bubbly. About 15 minutes. Serves 4. Great with vanilla ice cream.

CAKES & PIES

*Opportunity may knock once, but temptation
bangs on your front door forever.*

Blueberry Cream Cheese Coffeecake

1/2 cup butter, softened
1-1/4 cups sugar
2 eggs
1 teaspoon grated lemon peel
2-1/4 cups all-purpose flour, divided
3 teaspoons baking powder
1 teaspoon salt
3/4 cup milk
1/4 cup water
2 cups fresh or frozen blueberries (do not thaw)
1 8-ounce package cream cheese, diced

Topping:
1/4 cup all-purpose flour
1/4 cup sugar
1 teaspoon grated lemon peel
2 tablespoons cold butter

In a large mixing bowl, cream butter and sugar. Add eggs one at a time beating well after each addition. Beat in lemon peel. Combine 2 cups flour, baking powder and salt. Add to the creamed mixture alternately with milk and water. In a bowl toss blueberries with remaining flour. Fold into batter along with cream cheese. Pour into a greased 13 x 9 x 2 inch baking pan. For topping combine the flour, sugar and lemon peel. Cut in butter until the mixture is crumbly. Sprinkle over the batter. Bake at 375° for 35-40 minutes or until a toothpick inserted near the center comes out clean. Cool completely on a wire rack. Serves 15.

Blueberry Upside Down Cake

1/4 cup butter or margarine
1/2 cup sugar
2 cups fresh or frozen blueberries
2 teaspoons grated lemon peel, divided
1 8 1/2-ounce package yellow cake mix
1/2 cup heavy cream whipped or Cool Whip®

Melt the butter in an 8 inch square baking pan. Sprinkle sugar evenly over the butter. Mix the blueberries and 1 teaspoon lemon peel. Sprinkle the blueberries over the sugar. Prepare the cake mix according to the package directions, stirring in the remaining 1 teaspoon lemon peel at the end of mixing. Spread the batter over the berries. Bake in a 375° oven for 30 minutes or until the cake tests done. Let stand 10 minutes. Turn out on a platter. Serve warm. Top with whipped cream if desired.

Blueberry Cheesecake

Crust:
1 cup graham cracker crumbs
3 teaspoons sugar
3 tablespoons melted butter

Cheesecake:
2 8-ounce packages cream cheese
3/4 cup sugar
1/4 cup flour
2 eggs
1 cup evaporated milk
1-1/2 teaspoons vanilla

Blueberry Topping:
3 cups fresh blueberries
1/4 cup water
1/4 teaspoon nutmeg
1 cup sugar
2 teaspoons butter
2 tablespoons cornstarch
2 tablespoons lemon juice

Mix the crust ingredients together until blended. Press the mixture into the bottom of a 9 inch spring form pan. Bake at 325° for 10 minutes. Meanwhile prepare filling by creaming cheese with a mixer. Add the sugar, flour and eggs one at a time. Beat this until smooth. Add the evaporated milk and vanilla. Mix until blended. Pour slowly over the crust. Bake at 325° for 40 minutes. Remove to cooling rack. Prepare topping by combining the blueberries, water, nutmeg and sugar in a saucepan. Cook until blueberries are tender. Add the butter. Dissolve the cornstarch in the lemon juice and add to the blueberries. Cook until the mixture thickens, about 2-3 minutes, cool. Spread over the cheesecake and refrigerate until time to serve.

Almond Blueberry Coffeecake

3/4 cup butter or margarine, softened
1 cup sugar
4 eggs
2 teaspoons lemon juice
1-3/4 cups flour
2 teaspoons baking powder
2 cups fresh blueberries
2 teaspoons lemon juice
almond topping

Almond Topping:
1 cup flour
1/4 cup sugar
1/2 cup slivered almonds,
   toasted
1/4 cup butter or margarine

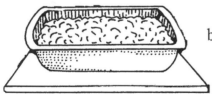

Cream softened butter. Gradually add sugar beating until light and fluffy. Add eggs one at a time beating well after each addition. Next stir in 2 teaspoons lemon juice. Combine flour and baking powder. Stir into creamed mixture, mixing well. Spread batter evenly in a greased and floured 13 x 9 x 2 inch glass baking dish. Sprinkle with blueberries and 2 teaspoons lemon juice.

For topping combine the flour, sugar and almonds. Cut in butter until mixture resembles coarse meal. Sprinkle topping on cake. Bake at 325° for 40 to 45 minutes. Serves 15.

Blueberry Loaf Cake

1/2 cup butter or margarine, softened
1 cup sugar
2 eggs
1/2 cup milk
1 teaspoon vanilla extract
1-3/4 cups flour
1 teaspoon baking powder
1 cup fresh or frozen blueberries

Topping:
2 teaspoons sugar
1 teaspoon ground cinnamon

In a mixing bowl, cream butter and sugar. Beat in the eggs, milk and vanilla. Combine flour and baking powder. Add to creamed mixture. Gently fold in the blueberries. Pour into a greased loaf pan. Combine sugar and cinnamon, sprinkle over the top. Bake at 350° for 50-55 minutes or until a toothpick is inserted near the center and it comes out clean. Cool for 10 minutes before removing from pan to a wire rack to cool.

Easy Individual Cheesecakes

14 vanilla wafers
12 ounces cream cheese, softened
2/3 cup sugar
2 eggs
1 teaspoon vanilla extract
3/4 cup sour cream
1/4 cup sugar
1 10-ounce package frozen blueberries thawed and drained

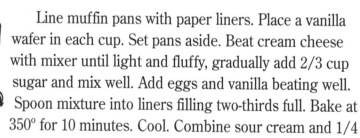

Line muffin pans with paper liners. Place a vanilla wafer in each cup. Set pans aside. Beat cream cheese with mixer until light and fluffy, gradually add 2/3 cup sugar and mix well. Add eggs and vanilla beating well. Spoon mixture into liners filling two-thirds full. Bake at 350° for 10 minutes. Cool. Combine sour cream and 1/4 cup sugar. Mix well. Spread over each with a heaping teaspoonful of blueberries. Freeze 5 minutes before serving.

Fruit Filled Coffeecake

1 cup oil
1 cup sugar
4 eggs
1 teaspoon vanilla
2 cups flour
1 teaspoon baking soda
1 can blueberry pie filling

Mix by hand. Stir oil, sugar, eggs and vanilla together. Add the dry ingredients. Spread half of this mixture into a 9 x 13 inch pan. Spread the pie filling over the first layer. Spread remaining batter over the top. Bake at 350° for about 30 minutes. Do not over bake. When cooled, top with powdered sugar frosting.

Fruit Topped Angel Cake

1 cup canned cherry pie filling
1 cup strawberries, sliced
1 cup blueberries
1 cup cantaloupe, cubed
1 cup pineapple, chopped
1 large banana, sliced
1 pint any flavor sherbet, softened
12 slices angel food cake, 1 inch thick
whipped topping
whole strawberries

In a large bowl, carefully stir together pie filling, the sliced strawberries, blueberries, cantaloupe, pineapple and banana. To serve spread some of the sherbet over each piece of cake. Top with fruit mixture and garnish with whipped topping and whole strawberries. Makes 12 servings.

Sour Cream Berry Cake

1 cup butter or margarine, softened
1-1/4 cups sugar
2 eggs
1 cup (8 ounces) sour cream
1 teaspoon vanilla extract
2 cups flour
1 teaspoon baking powder
1/2 teaspoon baking soda
2 cups raspberries
1 cup blueberries

Glaze:
2 cups confectioners sugar
1/4 cup butter or margarine,
  melted
1/2 teaspoon vanilla extract
2-3 tablespoons milk

In a mixing bowl cream butter and sugar. Add the eggs, sour cream and vanilla. Mix well. Combine the flour, baking powder and baking soda. Gradually add to creamed mixture. Spread into a greased 9 x 13 x 2 inch baking pan. Sprinkle the berries over the batter. Bake at 325° for 40 to 45 minutes or until a toothpick inserted comes out clean.

For the glaze: In a mixing bowl beat confectioners sugar, butter, extract and enough milk to achieve drizzle. Drizzle glaze over warm cake and cool on wire rack.

Blueberry Coffeecake

2 cups flour
1/2 cup sugar
1 tablespoon baking powder
1/2 teaspoon salt
1/2 teaspoon ground ginger
1/4 teaspoon baking soda
1/2 cup shortening
2 eggs, beaten
1/2 cup buttermilk or sour milk
2 cups fresh or frozen blueberries

Streusel topping:
1/2 cup packed brown sugar
1/4 cup flour
1/4 teaspoon ground ginger
2 tablespoons butter or margarine

Stir together the first 6 ingredients, cut in shortening until crumbly. Combine eggs and buttermilk. Add to crumbly mixture. Beat well. Spread batter in a greased 13 x 9 x 2 inch baking pan. Top with berries.

For streusel topping, combine brown sugar, flour, and ginger. Cut in butter or margarine until mixture is crumbly. Sprinkle streusel topping over blueberries. Bake at 350° for 30 to 35 minutes. Serve warm or cool.

Blueberry Cake

3 cups flour
2 cups sugar
1 teaspoon salt
1 teaspoon ground nutmeg
1 teaspoon ground cinnamon
1 teaspoon ground cloves
3 eggs, beaten
1 cup butter, melted
1 cup buttermilk
1-1/2 cups fresh blueberries
1 tablespoon baking soda
1/2 cup pecans, chopped
1/2 cup raisins

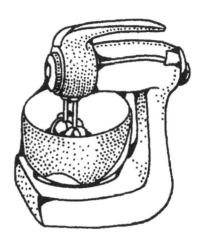

Combine flour, sugar, salt, nutmeg, cinnamon and cloves in a large mixing bowl. Add eggs, butter, buttermilk and blueberries. Beat for 1 minute at medium speed. Stir in soda, pecans and raisins. Spoon batter into greased and floured 10 inch tube pan. Bake at 350° for 55-60 minutes or until cake tests done.

Blueberry Bunt Cake and Sauce

Blueberry Cake:
3 cups cake flour
2-1/2 teaspoons baking powder
1/4 teaspoon salt
1-1/4 cups (2-1/2 sticks) unsalted butter at room temperature
1-3/4 cups sugar
4 eggs
1 tablespoon grated lemon rind
2 teaspoons vanilla
1 cup lemonade
1-1/2 cups blueberries

Blueberry Sauce:
1 cup blueberries
1/4 cup sugar
2 teaspoons cornstarch
1/4 cup water

Blueberry Bunt Cake and Sauce Continued

Preheat oven to 350°. Spray your bunt pan with nonstick cooking spray. Sift together first 3 ingredients into a bowl. In a bowl with an electric mixer, beat the butter until smooth, then add the sugar beating until light and fluffy. Beat in the eggs one at a time. Stir in lemon rind and vanilla. Alternately beat in the flour mixture and lemonade in 3 batches into the butter mixture, mix until incorporated. Fold in the blueberries. Scrape the batter into the prepared pan. Bake for 45 to 50 minutes or until the top is golden and a wooden pick inserted in the center comes out clean.

Prepare sauce: combine blueberries, sugar, cornstarch and water in a medium size saucepan. Cook over medium heat until sugar is dissolved, the liquid is clear and the blueberries begin to burst, about 5 to 7 minutes. Transfer mixture to food processor or blender. Puree until smooth. Let cool. To serve cut cake into slices and drizzle with warm or room temperature blueberry sauce.

Nut Topped Coffeecake

Filling:
4 cups blueberries
1 cup water
2 teaspoons lemon juice
1 cup sugar
1/3 cup cornstarch

Cake:
3 cups flour
1 cup sugar
1 tablespoon baking powder
1 teaspoon salt
1 teaspoon cinnamon
1/4 teaspoon nutmeg
1 cup margarine
2 eggs
1 cup milk
1 teaspoon vanilla

Topping:
1/2 cup sugar
1/2 cup flour
1/4 cup margarine
1/4 cup nuts, chopped

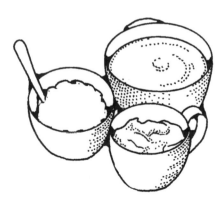

Nut Topped Coffeecake Continued

Filling: combine fruit with water and simmer covered for 5 minutes. Add lemon juice. Mix sugar and cornstarch and add to the fruit, stirring until thickened. Cool.

Cake: combine flour, sugar, baking powder, salt, cinnamon and nutmeg. Cut in margarine until mixture is fine crumbs. Combine eggs, milk and vanilla. Add to dry ingredients mixing until blended. Spread half in a greased 9 x 13 inch pan. Spoon the fruit filling over the batter, then the remaining batter over the fruit filling.

Topping: combine ingredients. Sprinkle over the batter and bake at 350º for 45 to 50 minutes

Cranberry Blueberry Pie

Pastry for 2 crust pie
1 cup sugar
3 tablespoons cornstarch
dash of salt
2 cups blueberries
1-1/2 cups whole cranberries

In a bowl, combine the sugar, cornstarch and salt. Stir in the berries until coated. Pour the berry mixture into a 9 inch pastry line pie tin. Adjust the top crust. Seal and crimp the edges of the pastry. Cut vents on top of the pastry. Bake in a 425° oven for 40 to 50 minutes until pastry is lightly browned and juices bubble through the vents. You can place tin foil around the pie pastry edges to prevent burning. Remove 10 minutes before the pie is done to brown the edges.

Blueberry Pie

Pastry for 2 crust pie
4 cups blueberries
1 cup sugar
3 tablespoons quick cooking tapioca
1/4 teaspoon salt
1/4 teaspoon cinnamon
2 tablespoons butter
2 tablespoons sugar
1 teaspoon lemon juice

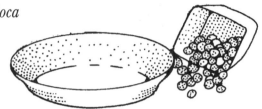

Line a pie pan with one pastry crust. In a bowl combine the blueberries, 1 cup sugar, tapioca, salt and cinnamon. Place this mixture into the pie shell. In a small bowl combine the butter, remaining sugar and lemon juice. Sprinkle this over the blueberry mixture. Cover with remaining pie pastry. Seal the edges, slit the pastry top to vent. Bake at 400° for 45 minutes. You can cover the pastry edges with foil to prevent over browned crust edges. Remove foil for 10 minutes before pie is done.

Berry Cheese Pie

1 pint fresh strawberries, sliced and divided
1 tablespoon lemon juice
2/3 cup sugar divided
1 8-ounce package cream cheese, softened
1 teaspoon grated lemon peel
1 9 inch graham cracker crust
2 tablespoons cornstarch
3-4 drops red food coloring, optional
1 pint fresh blueberries

In a bowl, combine half of the strawberries and lemon juice, mash the berries. Add 1/3 cup plus 2 tablespoons sugar, set aside. In a mixing bowl combine the cream cheese, lemon peel and remaining sugar. Spread into the crust. In a saucepan combine the cornstarch and reserved strawberry mixture until blended. Bring to a boil and stir for 2 minutes. Stir in food coloring if desired. Cool slightly. Fold in blueberries and remaining strawberries. Spread over cream cheese mixture. Cover and refrigerate for at least 3 hours.

Blueberry Apple Pie

3/4 cup sugar
2 tablespoons tapioca
1/2 teaspoon ground cinnamon
3 cups cooking apples, peeled and thinly sliced
2 cups blueberries
1 tablespoon lemon juice
pastry for a double crust pie
1 tablespoon butter or margarine, cut up
whipped topping or vanilla ice cream

In a large bowl combine the sugar, tapioca and cinnamon. Add to this the apples, berries and lemon juice. Let stand for 20 minutes. Transfer the apple-berry mixture to a 9 inch pastry lined pie plate. Cut slits in the remaining pastry. Place on pie filling and seal, crimp the edges of pie and cover with foil. Bake at 375° for 25 minutes. Remove the foil and bake for 25-30 minutes more or until top is golden. Serve with whipped topping or ice cream.

French Blueberry Pie

1 9 inch pie shell, baked
2 3-ounce packages cream cheese, softened
2 tablespoons milk
1 teaspoon grated lemon peel
4 cups fresh or frozen blueberries
1 tablespoon lemon juice
1/8 teaspoon salt
water
1 cup sugar
2 tablespoons cornstarch

In a mixing bowl add the softened cream cheese, milk and lemon peel. Beat until smooth. Spread the cheese mixture evenly in the bottom of the baked pie shell. Sprinkle 2 cups of whole blueberries over the cheese layer. Mash the remainder of the blueberries. Place into a 2 cup measuring cup, add lemon juice, salt and enough water to make 1-1/2 cups of pulp and liquid. Place this into a saucepan. Mix the sugar and cornstarch. Stir this into the blueberry pulp. Bring to a boil, stirring constantly and cook for about 2 minutes or until thickened. Cool this mixture until it is luke warm. Spoon onto the blueberries. Chill pie for several hours.

Blueberry-Vanilla Pie

1 5-ounce package rolled sugar ice cream cones, crushed, about 1-1/2 cups
1/4 cup ground nuts, pecans or walnuts
1/3 cup butter or margarine, melted
3 cups blueberries, save some for garnish
1 quart vanilla ice cream, softened
whipped cream

In a medium mixing bowl, combine the crushed cones and ground nuts. Stir in melted butter. In a 10 inch pie plate, press the crumb mixture forming a pie crust. Place 2-1/2 cups of the blueberries into a blender or food processor, cover and blend or process until nearly smooth. In a large mixing bowl, stir together the blueberries puree, softened ice cream and remaining 1/2 cup blueberries. Freeze for about 30-45 minutes or until mixture mounds, stirring occasionally. Spoon into prepared crust. Cover and freeze about 8 hours or until firm. To serve, let pie stand at room temperature for about 15 minutes before cutting into wedges. Top each serving with whipped topping and extra blueberries.

Patriotic Pie

2 cups rhubarb, chopped
3/4 cup granulated sugar
5 tablespoons water
2 tablespoons cornstarch
2 cups strawberries, halved
1 8-ounce package cream cheese, softened
1/2 cup sifted powdered sugar
1 tablespoon milk
1 9 inch pastry shell, baked and cooled
whipped cream
blueberries

In medium saucepan combine rhubarb, granulated sugar and 3 tablespoons water. Bring to a boil, reduce heat. Cover and cook over medium-low heat for 5 minutes. Dissolve cornstarch in the remaining 2 tablespoons of water. Add strawberries and cornstarch mixture to rhubarb in saucepan. Cook and stir for 2 minutes. Cover and set aside without stirring for 30 minutes. Meanwhile in a small mixing bowl, beat cream cheese, powdered sugar and milk with an electric mixer until smooth. Spread in the pastry shell. Top with cool rhubarb mixture. Cover and chill at least 4 hours. Before serving top with whipped cream and sprinkle with the blueberries. Serves 8.

Chilled Blueberry Pie

3 cups blueberries
1-1/2 cups water
1/4 cup cornstarch
1/2 cup sugar
2 tablespoons honey
1 tablespoon lemon juice
1/4 teaspoon salt
1/4 teaspoon ground nutmeg
1 9 inch pastry shell, baked and cooled
Cool Whip®
Red raspberries

Place 1 cup of the blueberries in a large saucepan. Crush with a potato masher or fork. Combine water and cornstarch. Add to crushed blueberries, along with the sugar, honey, lemon juice, salt and nutmeg. Add remaining blueberries. Cook and stir until thickened and bubbly. Reduce heat, cook and stir for 2 minutes more. Pour hot mixture into pastry shell. Cover with plastic wrap and chill at least 6 hours or overnight. Just before serving, garnish with Cool Whip® and raspberries.

DESSERTS

For nothing is impossible with God. Luke 1:37.

Blueberry Swirls

1-1/2 to 2 cups frozen blueberries
1 cup sifted flour
4-1/2 tablespoons baking powder
1-1/2 teaspoons sugar plus 1 to 2 tablespoons
1/4 teaspoon salt
3 tablespoons oil
6 tablespoons milk
1 tablespoon melted butter
1-1/2 teaspoons quick cooking tapioca

Thaw blueberries, drain, reserve the liquid. In a bowl combine flour, baking powder, 1-1/2 teaspoons sugar and salt thoroughly. Blend in the oil. Add milk gradually to form a soft dough. Place dough on a lightly floured board. Roll out to a 1/2 inch thick rectangle. Brush with butter, spread evenly with berries. Sprinkle with remaining sugar. Roll up from longer side. With a greased knife cut dough into six slices. In a pot combine blueberry liquid and tapioca. Bring to a boil. Cook for 2 minutes, stirring often. Pour into baking pan. Top with slices. Bake at 425° for 25 to 30 minutes, until golden brown. Serves 6.

Chocolate Blueberry Clusters

2 cups (11-1/2 ounces) milk chocolate chips
1/4 cup butter or margarine
2 cups fresh blueberries
1-1/2 inch paper candy liners

Over hot, not boiling, water, combine the chocolate chips and butter in a double boiler. Stir until melted and the mixture is smooth. Remove from heat. Place 1 teaspoon of melted chocolate in paper candy liners. Add 6-8 blueberries. Top with 2 teaspoons chocolate making sure the blueberries are well coated. Chill for 20-30 minutes. Serve at room temperature. Store in refrigerator. Makes 2-1/2 dozen.

Blueberry Peach Truffle

1 14-ounce can sweetened condensed milk
1-1/2 cups cold water
2 teaspoons grated lemon rind
1 3-1/2 ounce package instant vanilla pudding, prepared
2 cups whipping cream, whipped
4 cups pound cake, cut into 3/4 inch cubes
2-1/2 cups fresh peaches or nectarines
2 cups fresh or frozen blueberries, well drained
4 quart glass bowl

Combine condensed milk, water and lemon rind in a large bowl, mix well. Add pudding mix, beat until well blended. Chill 5 minutes. Fold in whipped cream. Spoon 2 cups pudding mix into glass serving bowl. Top with 1/2 of cake cubes and all of the peaches. Layer 1/2 of the remaining pudding mix, then remaining cake cubes, blueberries and remaining pudding mixture. Spread to about 1 inch from side of bowl. Chill about 4 hours. Serves 20.

Berry Dessert

Lorraine Beal, my friend in Christ who is an awesome cook donated this recipe.

Crust:

1 cup walnuts or pecans, processed fine
1 cup butter or margarine, melted
2 cups flour

Mix crust ingredients, press into a 9 x 13 inch pan and bake at 350° for 20-23 minutes. Let cool.

Center:

1 8-ounce package cream cheese, softened
1 cup powdered sugar
1 8-ounce carton of regular Cool Whip® or Strawberry flavored Cool Whip®.

Mix cream cheese and powdered sugar until well blended. Fold in Cool Whip® and spread this mixture over the baked crust.

Topping:

Use fresh blueberries, raspberries, blackberries or any other fruit to cover the top. Don't use frozen fruit unless you thicken it.

Blueberry-Lemon Chiffon Dessert

1-1/2 cups graham cracker crumbs, about 24 squares
1-1/3 cups sugar, divided
1/2 cup butter, melted
1-1/2 cups fresh blueberries, divided
1 3-ounce package lemon gelatin
1 cup boiling water
2 8-ounce packages and one 3-ounce package cream cheese, softened
1 teaspoon vanilla extract
1 16-ounce carton Cool Whip®

In a small bowl, combine the cracker crumbs, 1/3 cup sugar and butter, set aside 2 tablespoons for topping. Press the remaining crumb mixture into a 13 x 9 x 2 pan. Sprinkle with 1 cup blueberries. In a small bowl dissolve gelatin in boiling water, cool. In a large mixing bowl, beat cream cheese and remaining sugar. Add vanilla, mix well. Slowly add dissolved gelatin. Fold in Cool Whip®. Spread over blueberries. Sprinkle with reserved crumb mixture and remaining blueberries. Cover and refrigerate for 3 hours or until set. Refrigerate leftovers. Serves 12-15.

Blueberry Vanilla Truffle

2 cups milk
1 3-ounce package cook and serve vanilla pudding mix
1 10-3/4 ounce loaf pound cake
1/4 cup blueberry jam
1/4 cup orange juice
10 macaroon cookies
2 cups blueberries
1 cup heavy whipping cream
2 tablespoons confectioners sugar
1/4 cup sliced almonds, toasted

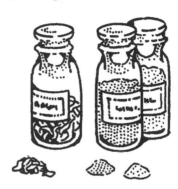

In a small saucepan, combine milk and pudding mix. Cook and stir over medium heat until mixture comes to a full boil. Cool. Spread the top of the pound cake with jam and cut into 1 inch cubes. Place cubes, jam side up, in a 3-quart truffle or glass bowl. Drizzle with orange juice. Place macaroons in a food processor or blender. Cover and process until coarse crumbs form. Set aside 1/4 cup crumbs for garnish. Sprinkle remaining crumbs over cake cubes. Top with berries and pudding. Cover and refrigerate overnight. Just before serving, in a small mixing bowl beat cream until thickened. Beat in confectioner's sugar until stiff peaks form. Spread over truffle. Sprinkle with almonds and remaining macaroon crumbs. Serves 10-12.

Blueberry-Lemon Parfait

2 cups blueberries fresh or frozen
2 8-ounce cartons lemon yogurt
10 gingersnaps, crumbled

Take four parfait or tall glasses, layer 1/2 cup blueberries, 1/2 cup yogurt, then crumbled gingersnaps into each glass.

Wild Blueberry Dessert

1-3/4 cups flour
1-1/2 teaspoons baking powder
1/2 teaspoon baking soda
1/2 teaspoon salt
1/4 cup shortening
1 cup sugar
1 egg
3/4 cup milk
1-1/2 cups wild blueberries
1/2 cup chopped walnuts

Sauce:
1/2 cup sugar
2 tablespoons cornstarch
1-3/4 cups apple juice
2 tablespoons butter or margarine
1/4 teaspoon almond extract
1/2 cup wild blueberries
whipped cream
extra blueberries for garnish if desired

Wild Blueberry Dessert Continued

In a medium bowl, stir together the flour, baking powder, baking soda and salt, set aside. In a large mixing bowl, beat together the shortening, 1 cup sugar, egg and milk until well combined, add the flour mixture and stir. Stir in the 1-1/2 cups blueberries and the nuts. Pour mixture into a greased 9 x 9 x 2 baking pan. Bake at 350° for 35-40 minutes or until toothpick test clean. For sauce, in a medium saucepan combine 1/2 cup sugar and the cornstarch. Stir in the apple juice. Bringing mixture to boiling, stir constantly. Reduce heat, cook and stir for 2 minutes. Remove from heat and stir in the butter or margarine, almond extract and 1/2 cup blueberries. To serve, spoon warm sauce over a dessert serving. Garnish with whipped cream and blueberries.

Fruit On A Cloud

1/2 cup whipped topping
1/3 cup sour cream
1/3 cup powdered sugar
whipped topping
1 cup sliced strawberries
1 cup blueberries
1 small banana
1 kiwi fruit, peeled and thinly sliced
1/4 cup sliced almonds
ground cinnamon

In a small bowl, combine 1/2 cup whipped topping, sour cream and powdered sugar, set aside. In the bottom of 4 dessert dishes, place a generous mound of whipped topping. Layer the fruits in the dishes alternately with the sour cream mixture and sliced almonds. Top with more whipped topping. Sprinkle with cinnamon. Serves 4.

Blueberry Tiramisu

1 3-ounce package cream cheese, softened
1 cup ricotta cheese
1/3 cup frozen orange juice concentrate, thawed
1 can vanilla or lemon pudding
2 3-ounce packages ladyfingers, split
3 cups blueberries
1 cup raspberries
whipped cream

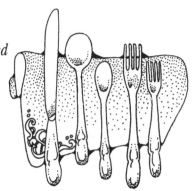

In a mixing bowl, combine cream cheese, ricotta cheese and orange juice concentrate. Add pudding, stirring until smooth. Arrange half of the ladyfingers cut side up, in a 2-quart rectangle baking dish. Spoon half of the pudding mixture evenly on top. Sprinkle with half of the blueberries and raspberries. Repeat layers. Cover and chill at least 4 hours or overnight. To serve cut into pieces. Garnish with whipped topping. Serves 12.

Blueberry Oatmeal Dessert

1/4 cup sugar
2 tablespoons cornstarch
1/3 cup water
1 teaspoon lemon juice
2-1/2 cups blueberries fresh or frozen
1 package yellow cake mix
1-1/2 cups quick cooking oats, divided
8 tablespoons cold butter, divided
2 eggs
1/4 cup packed brown sugar

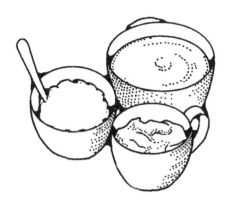

In a saucepan, combine sugar and cornstarch. Gradually whisk in water and lemon juice until smooth. Stir in blueberries. Cook and stir longer or until thickened and bubbly. Remove from heat and set aside. In a bowl combine the dry cake mix and one cup oats. Cut in 6 tablespoons butter until crumbly. Set aside 1 cup crumb mixture for topping. Stir eggs into remaining crumb mixture. Press into a greased 13 x 9 x 2 inch baking dish. Spread blueberry mixture to within 1/4 inch of edges. Combine the brown sugar, remaining oats and reserved crumb mixture. Cut in remaining butter until crumbly. Sprinkle over the top. Bake at 350° for 30-35 minutes or until golden brown. Serve warm with whipped topping or ice cream.

Blueberry Delight

24 squares or 1 package (12) graham crackers
2 packages dream whip
1 cup cold milk
1 teaspoon vanilla
1 cup powdered sugar
1 8-ounce package cream cheese, softened
1 can blueberries, drain off juice

Roll crackers until crumbs and put half in the bottom of a 8 x 8 cake pan. Mix 2 packages of dream whip with 1 cup of milk and vanilla into a large bowl, beat until thick. Add powdered sugar and cream cheese, beat until real stiff. Put half of this on top of the cracker crumbs in the pan. Put the can of berries on next, then the rest of the dream whip mixture. Sprinkle the rest of the cracker crumbs on next. Put in the refrigerator, chill.

Berry Parfaits

1 tablespoon sugar
1 teaspoon finely shredded orange peel
1/2 teaspoon finely shredded lemon peel
1/8 teaspoon ground cinnamon
dash of salt
1 8-ounce carton plain yogurt
1-1/2 cups sliced strawberries
1-1/2 cups blueberries

In a bowl combine the sugar, orange and lemon peel, cinnamon and salt. Gently fold in the yogurt. Set aside 6 strawberry slices and 6 blueberries. In 6 parfait glasses layer the remaining strawberries, yogurt mixture and blueberries. Top berries with a dallop of yogurt mixture. Place a strawberry slice and blueberry on top of each parfait.

Blueberry Orange Sherbet

1/3 cup orange marmalade
1 pint orange sherbet
1 cup fresh blueberries

Heat the marmalade over low heat until melted in a saucepan. Scoop sherbet into 4 dessert dishes. Top with the blueberries. Spoon the warm marmalade over the berries and sherbet.

Frozen Blueberry Fluff
This should be prepared a day ahead of time.

1-1/4 cup crisp cookie crumbs
1/3 cup butter
2 egg whites
1 tablespoon lemon juice
1-1/3 cup sugar
2 cups fresh blueberries
1 cup heavy cream, whipped

In a bowl, mix the crumbs and butter. Press into the bottom of a buttered 9 inch square pan or a 7 inch round spring form pan. Bake in a 350° oven for 8 minutes and cool. In a mixing bowl beat the egg whites and lemon juice slightly. Then add the sugar and blueberries. Beat on high for 12-15 minutes until the mixture is fluffy and has larger volume. Fold in the whipped cream. Spread over the crumb crust. Freeze overnight. Garnish with fresh berries.

Blueberry Puffball

This is by my son Michael (Mike) Bestwick.

1 quart strawberries, sliced
1/3 cup sugar
1-1/2 pints blueberries
1 small package vanilla pudding
1/2 angel food cake, cut up into chunks
Cool Whip®

In a bowl, combine the strawberries and sugar. Let sit for a few hours so that the mixture juices up. Meanwhile, mix the pudding according to package directions and chill. When ready to assemble, get a medium size bowl. Place a layer of cake cubes, then 1/2 the strawberries and toss gently. Next put in 1/2 the pudding and 1/2 of the blueberries. Repeat the layers and let set for about 15 minutes so that the juices can soak into the cake. Spoon into serving bowls and top with Cool Whip®.

Blueberry Crumb Pudding

1 cup cinnamon graham cracker crumbs
1/4 cup sugar
3 tablespoons butter
2 cups fresh blueberries

Combine the graham cracker crumbs and sugar into a bowl and mix. Cut the butter into this mixture. In an 8 x 8 inch pan, place 1 cup of blueberries and cover with 1/2 of the crumb mixture, repeat. Bake at 350° for 30 minutes. Cut into squares and serve warm. Top with vanilla ice cream or Cool Whip®. Serves 6.

Fruit In Vanilla Sauce With Biscuits

1 8-ounce package biscuit mix
2 teaspoons vanilla
2 teaspoons sugar
1/2 cup water
3 tablespoons sugar
2 teaspoons vanilla
3 cups coarsely chopped fruit, 1 cup blueberries, 1 cup kiwi fruit
    and 1 cup strawberries
whipped cream

Prepare biscuit dough according to package directions for rolled biscuits adding 2 teaspoons vanilla to the dough. Roll or pat the dough into a 6 inch circle and cut into 6 wedges. Place wedges on a baking sheet. Moisten tops with a little water and sprinkle with 2 teaspoons of sugar. Bake according to package directions. Meanwhile in a small saucepan, combine 1/2 cup water and 3 tablespoons sugar. Bring to a boil and reduce heat. Simmer uncovered for 5 minutes. Remove from heat and stir in the remaining 2 teaspoons vanilla. Cool slightly. Pour the syrup over the fruit. Toss gently to coat. To serve carefully split the warm biscuits wedges in half horizontally. Place bottom portions on 6 dessert plates. Spoon some of the fruit mixture and syrup over each portion. Top with biscuit wedges and whipped cream. Serves 6.

Strawberry-Blueberry Cream Tarts

2 packages (6 count each) individual graham cracker tart shells
2 egg whites, beaten
1 cup sugar
1/2 cup plus 2 tablespoons flour
3 cups milk
2 eggs, beaten
6 tablespoons butter or margarine, cubed
2 tablespoons lemon juice
12 medium strawberries, sliced
12 blueberries
6 tablespoons strawberry jelly, melted

Brush insides of tart shells with egg whites. Place on two baking sheets. Bake at 350° for 5 minutes. Cool completely on wire racks. In a heavy saucepan, combine the sugar and flour. Gradually stir in milk until smooth. Bring to a boil over medium heat stirring constantly. Cook and stir for 1 minute. Remove from heat. Stir a small amount of hot milk mixture into eggs. Return all to the pan, stirring constantly. Bring to a gentle boil. Cook and stir for 1 minute. Remove from the heat. Stir in butter and lemon juice. Refrigerate until chilled. Just before serving, spoon custard into shells. Top with strawberries and blueberries. Spoon jelly over the fruit.

WHAT NOTS

Don't let your worries get the best of you.

ABC Dumplings

1 cup peeled, cored, chopped tart apples
1 cup fresh or frozen blueberries
3/4 cup fresh or frozen cranberries
1 cup water
2/3 cup sugar

Dumplings:
3/4 cup flour
1/4 cup sugar
1 teaspoon baking powder
1/4 teaspoon ground cinnamon
1/8 teaspoon ground nutmeg
3 tablespoons cold butter or margarine
1/3 cup milk

In a saucepan, combine the fruit, water and sugar. Bring to a boil. Reduce heat, cover and simmer for 5 minutes. Meanwhile, in a bowl combine the flour, sugar, baking powder, cinnamon and nutmeg. Cut in the butter until the mixture resembles coarse crumbs. Add the milk, stir just until moistened. Drop into six mounds onto simmering fruit. Cover and simmer for about 10 minutes or until a toothpick inserted into a dumpling comes out clean. DO NOT LIFT COVER WHILE SIMMERING! You can serve with half-and-half or Cool Whip®.

Frozen Soda Pop Fruit Cups

2 11-ounce cans Mandarin oranges, undrained
1 20-ounce can crushed pineapple, undrained
5 medium bananas, sliced
1-1/2 cups strawberries, fresh or frozen
1-1/2 cups blueberries, fresh or frozen
1 12-ounce can lemon-lime soda
1 cup water
3/4 cup lemonade concentrate
1/2 cup sugar

In a large bowl, combine all ingredients. Fill twenty 8-ounce plastic cups three-fourths full. Cover and freeze for 4 hours or until solid. Remove from freezer 30 minutes before serving. Makes 20 servings.

Lemon Blueberry Gelatin Mold

First Layer
1 3-ounce grape or lemon flavored gelatin
1/4 teaspoon salt
1-1/4 cups boiling water
1/2 cup grape juice
1 cup fresh or frozen unsweetened blueberries

Second Layer
1 3-ounce package lemon flavored gelatin
1 cup boiling water
1/2 cup cold water
2 tablespoons lemon juice
2 3-ounce packages cream cheese
3/4 cup creamed cottage cheese

To prepare first layer, dissolve the gelatin and salt in boiling water. Stir in the grape juice, chill until partially set. Fold in the blueberries and pour into a 6 cup mold and chill until firm. To prepare the second layer, dissolve gelatin in the 1 cup boiling water. Add cold water and lemon juice. Chill just until cooled and syrupy. Beat the cream cheese and cottage cheese until softened. Add cooled gelatin to the cheese mixture and beat until light. Pour over the blueberry mixture. Chill until firm. Unmold, serves 6.

Chilled Blueberry Soup

1/2 cup sugar
2 tablespoons cornstarch
2-3/4 cups water
2 cups blueberries
1 cinnamon stick, 3 inches
1 6-ounce can frozen orange juice concentrate
sour cream, optional

In a large saucepan combine sugar and cornstarch. Gradually stir in water until smooth. Bring to a boil over medium heat. Cook and stir for 2 minutes or until thickened. Add blueberries and cinnamon stick, return to a boil. Remove from the heat. Stir in orange juice concentrate until melted. Cover and refrigerate for at least 1 hour. Discard cinnamon stick. Garnish with sour cream if desired.

Blueberry-Plum Cups

2-1/2 cups fresh purple plums, pitted and sliced
2-1/2 cups fresh blueberries
1/4 cup firmly packed brown sugar
1 cup flour
1/3 cup sugar
1/3 cup firmly packed brown sugar
1/2 teaspoon salt
1/4 teaspoon nutmeg
1 egg
2 tablespoons margarine or butter, melted

Heat oven to 375°. Grease an 8 x 8 pan. In a medium bowl gently combine plums, blueberries and 1/4 cup brown sugar. Spoon about 1/2 cup fruit mixture into the pan. In a medium bowl combine flour, sugar, 1/3 cup brown sugar, salt and nutmeg. Mix well. Add egg and mix until crumbly. Sprinkle flour over fruit mixture and drizzle melted margarine over the flour mixture. Bake at 375° for 25 to 30 minutes or until topping is golden brown. Serve warm with ice cream.

Blueberry Kiwi Flan

Buy a prepared flan crust

Cream cheese filling:
1 8-ounce package cream cheese
1/3 cup sugar
1 teaspoon vanilla

Fruit layer:
3 cups blueberries
2 kiwi fruit, peeled and sliced thin

Citrus glaze:
1/2 cup water
1/2 cup orange juice
2 tablespoons lemon juice
1/4 cup granulated sugar
1 tablespoon cornstarch

In a bowl, cream together the cheese filling ingredients with a mixer. When mixed spread the filling ingredients on the crust. Place the blueberries and kiwi on top of the cheese layer in a decorative pattern. Refrigerate. To make the glaze combine all the ingredients in a saucepan. Bring to a boil, and boil 1 minute and then cool. Spread over the fruit layer, refrigerate until serving time.

Nutty Granola With Dried Blueberries

1/3 cup margarine, melted
3-4 tablespoons honey
3 tablespoons brown sugar
3 cups rolled oats
1/3 cup wheat cereal
1/3 cup raw sunflower seeds
1 teaspoon cinnamon, a dash more if desired
1/2 cup sliced almonds
1 teaspoon almond extract
1/2 teaspoon vanilla extract
1/4 cup walnuts
1/4 cup pecans
3/4 to 1 cup dried blueberries

In a 9 x 13 inch baking pan, stir together margarine, honey and brown sugar. Mix the rolled oats, cereal, sunflower seeds and cinnamon. Bake in oven at 350° for 15 minutes. Stir in the nuts and extracts. Bake 10 more minutes or until golden brown. Remove from oven and then stir in the dried blueberries. Cool, mix and store in an airtight container.

INDEX

*Cooking is like advice, you should try
it before you feed it to others.*

ISBN 0-932212-94-8

Look for Joan Bestwick's *Life's Little Zucchini Cookbook, Life's Little Rhubarb Cookbook, Life's Little Berry Cookbook, Life's Little Peaches, Pears, Plums & Prunes Cookbook* and *Life's Little Apple Cookbook* also by Avery Color Studios, Inc.

ISBN 1-892384-00-0

ISBN 1-892384-11-6

ISBN 1-892384-05-1

ISBN 1-892384-22-1

Avery Color Studios, Inc. has a full line of Great Lakes oriented books, puzzles, cookbooks, shipwreck and lighthouse maps, and lighthouse posters.

For a full color catalog call:
1-800-722-9925

Avery Color Studios, Inc. products are available at gift shops and bookstores throughout the Great Lakes region.